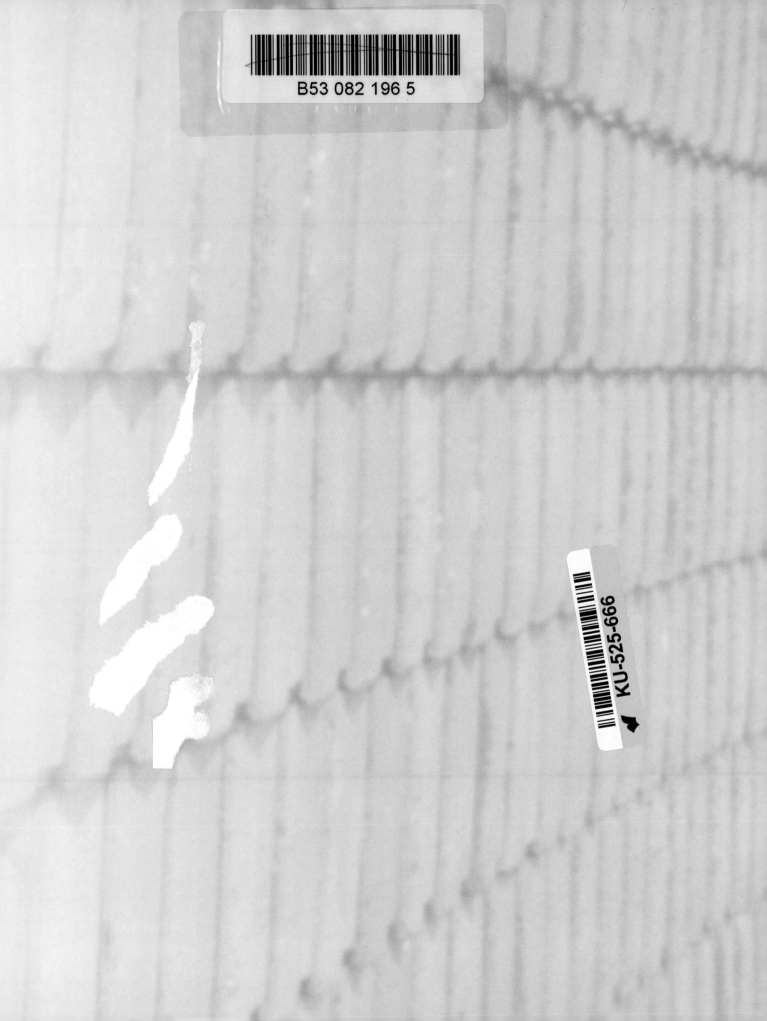

Heinz

Cath Senker

First published in 2014 by Wayland
Copyright © Wayland 2014

Wayland
338 Euston Road
London NW1 3BH

Wayland Australia
Level 17/207 Kent Street
Sydney, NSW 2000

Commissioning editor: Annabel Stones
Designer: LittleRedAnt (Anthony Hannant)
Picture researcher: Shelley Noronha

ISBN: 978 0 7502 8066 2
E-book ISBN: 978 0 7502 8552 0

Dewey categorisation: 338.7'61-dc23

Printed in China

10 9 8 7 6 5 4 3 2 1

Wayland is a division of Hachette Children's Books, an Hachette UK company.
www.hachette.co.uk

Picture acknowledgements: The author and publisher would like to thank the following
for allowing their pictures to be reproduced in this publication:
Cover: Shutterstock; title page: Shutterstock; p.4 (left and right) & p. 5: Shutterstock; p.6: Bettman/
Corbis; p.7: Topfoto; p.8: Thomas and Katherine Detre Library and Archives, Sen. John Heinz History
Center, Pittsburgh, PA; p.9: Heinz.com; p. 10 & p. 11: Thomas and Katherine Detre Library and
Archives, Sen. John Heinz History Center, Pittsburgh, PA; p. 12, left: Charles E. Rotkin/Corbis; p.12,
right: Heinz.com; p. 13: Spike Watson/ArenaPAL; p.14: Time & Life Pictures/Getty Images; p.15 Jones/
REX; p.16: TopFoto; p.17: David Crausby/Alamy; p.18: Bloomberg via Getty Images; p.19, bottom: AFP/
Getty Images; p. 19, top: TopFoto p.20: Shutterstock; p.21, bottom: Bill Johnson; p. 21, top: Heinz.com;
p.22 Topham/PA; p.23: Heinz.com; p.24: Getty Images; p.25: Shutterstock; p.26: Jason Cohn/Reuters/
Corbis; p.27: Brendan McDermid/Reuters/Corbis; p. 32: Comstock/Getty Images.

Contents

Heinz: king of ketchup

If you're eating a burger and chips, do you reach for the Heinz tomato ketchup to squirt on your meal? Perhaps you sometimes have Heinz baked beans for tea. A popular brand worldwide, Heinz is a major US manufacturer of processed foods.

With its headquarters in Pittsburgh, Pennsylvania, USA, Heinz sells its products in about 200 countries. In more than 50 of them, it enjoys the number-one or number-two market position. About half of its sales come from outside the USA.

Heinz makes more than 5,700 products – that's 100 times the '57 varieties' in its slogan! It has processing plants in several countries. Heinz's core products are Heinz Ketchup, Heinz Beanz (baked beans), Ore-Ida frozen potatoes, Weight Watchers meals and Classico pasta sauces. Heinz Ketchup is the best-known Heinz product. The company sells an astonishing 650 million bottles of ketchup each year. The special recipe for Heinz Ketchup is written in code, and just a few people are in on the secret.

Heinz produces its own tomato seeds so farmers can grow tomatoes for its products.

This book looks at the long history of Heinz, from its establishment nearly 150 years ago to its successful expansion into a global business and its takeover in 2013 by Berkshire Hathaway and 3G Capital. It looks at the key people who made the business flourish and the clever tactics they used to succeed.

Heinz is best known for its iconic tomato ketchup.

Business Matters

Heinz's most popular products worldwide

Ketchups and sauces

Heinz Ketchup

Classico pasta sauces

Lea & Perrins sauce

Salad cream

Pudliszki meals, snacks, ketchups and sauces

ABC soy sauce

Meals and snacks

Ore-Ida frozen potatoes

Bagel bites frozen potatoes

Delimex Mexican snacks

T.G.I. Fridays

Quality Chef frozen soups

Heinz Beanz

Honig soups and meals

Wattie's soups and sauces

BiAuglut gluten-free foods

Infant nutrition

Nurture infant formulas

Plasmon infant foods

Watties infant foods

It's said that a Heinz manager invented beans on toast in 1927 as a way to sell more beans.

Heinz starts out

Henry Heinz launched his first enterprise in 1869 in Sharpsburg, Pennsylvania, USA, with his colleague L. Clarence Noble. They sold horseradish, a popular condiment bottled and grated by Henry himself, sauerkraut (fermented cabbage) and pickles. But in 1875 the business went bust.

The young Heinz was lucky. His family provided money for him to start a new venture with two relatives in 1876, making tomato ketchup, pepper sauce and vinegar. Heinz's pickles were so popular that he became a household name, known as the 'pickle king'. This was unusual at the time; people did not generally know the names of food manufacturers.

In 1886, Heinz decided to sell his pickles and sauces abroad, so he travelled to England, proudly carrying samples. He visited the high-quality London store Fortnum and Mason. The owners loved his products and announced, 'I think Mr Heinz, we will take the lot.'

An early Heinz wagon transporting pickles and preserves.

The Heinz business in London, 1898, with a huge advertising slogan on the building front.

Despite his early success, Heinz knew he could not take sales for granted. The company followed a dual advertising strategy. Since people bought their food at grocers' shops, Heinz produced publicity to encourage grocers to recommend its products to customers. It also advertised to consumers, so that they would ask grocers to stock Heinz goods. Eye-catching signs were printed on the companies' buildings, boxes and vehicles and all products had a standard label, encouraging brand recognition.

Factory tours were another form of publicity. At the start of the twentieth century, 20,000 visitors toured Heinz factories annually, tasting samples of Heinz products at the end.

By 1905, Heinz was the largest producer of pickles, vinegar and ketchup in the USA. It was successful because of the growing market for prepared foods, its wide variety of products and lots of advertising.

The 'pickle king' – Henry John Heinz

Henry John Heinz (1844–1919) was born in Pittsburgh, Pennsylvania, USA, the son of German immigrants. A businessman at 16, he employed people to grow and deliver produce to grocers in Pittsburgh.

After the failure of Heinz's first business, he worked hard to make the new venture he set up in 1876 with his brother and a cousin more profitable. He came up with highly inventive marketing ideas. In 1896 Heinz was inspired by a shoe advertisement he saw while on a train, which stated it had '21 styles', and his famous '57 varieties' slogan was born.

Heinz became a major national enterprise by 1900. By the time of his death in 1919, the firm employed more than 6,000 workers and had 25 factories.

A lithograph (print of an illustration) showing the H. J. Heinz Company in Pittsburgh, USA around 1900.

Henry Heinz married Sarah Sloan Young Heinz in 1869 and they had four children.

Brains

Behind The Brand

Henry Heinz
Founder of Heinz

Heinz believed in doing business fairly. One of his mottos was 'deal with the seller so justly that he will want to sell to you again'. He treated his employees well and provided decent working conditions.

In the late nineteenth century, no laws existed to stop companies putting harmful substances in their products. But Heinz insisted that his factory production lines be kept clean and he advertised the purity of his products. In 1900 he set up a quality-control division with scientists to check the cleanliness of the manufacturing process. Heinz supported a national campaign for pure food, which led to the 1906 Federal Food and Drug Act.

In 1900, Heinz received two gold medals at the Paris Exhibition world fair, for product quality and for good factory conditions. He set a high standard for food manufacturing in the USA.

Heinz during Depression and war

In Heinz's first few decades, people made the products by hand. But from the early twentieth century, factories were built in the USA to make production quicker and easier. Heinz also set up factories abroad. It had been exporting its products to Britain, but in the 1920s, the company began production in the UK.

During the economic Depression of the early 1930s, many businesses failed but Heinz continued to do well. Heinz products were cheap enough for ordinary people to afford them, and the brand was popular. In 1931, Howard Heinz (Henry's son) added baby food and 'ready to serve' soups to the range.

He cleverly promoted the baby foods by asking doctors and nurses to give free samples to new mothers.

This Heinz factory in Pittsburgh, USA, made tin cans for baked beans, soup and other Heinz products.

Business Matters

Salesmen

From 1880 to 1920, salesmen used to visit grocery stores and fill up large jars with samples of Heinz products for customers to try, such as different flavours of vinegar. The salesmen served hot dishes too, such as baked beans and spaghetti. These demonstrations of products lasted for a week. The salesmen established a business relationship with store owners, and returned later with new products. They also brought promotional materials to leave at the shop, such as giant display pickles, to attract attention.

During the Second World War (1939–45), almost half of Heinz's production was for the Allied military forces. Heinz made C-rations for soldiers in combat, providing prepared meals such as meat and vegetable hash, and canned meals. K-rations were also produced; these were lightweight rations for paratroopers, who dropped into action from aircraft.

A smartly dressed Heinz travelling salesman promotes his products to a grocer.

In the UK, no Heinz Ketchup was made during the war since it was hard to import the ingredients because of battles at sea. The Heinz factory in Harlesden, London, was bombed, but production continued. It was still possible to make some goods to liven up home cooking, such as Salad Cream. Vinegar was popular too; people added it to vegetable dishes. The company introduced condensed soups to save tin. The soup was much thicker so the tins could be smaller, and consumers added water to thin the soup down.

11

New leadership, new businesses

In 1946, H. J. 'Jack' Heinz II made Heinz into a public company. Now people outside the Heinz family could buy shares and own a part of Heinz. He launched subsidiaries in Holland, Venezuela, Japan and Italy – companies controlled by Heinz that made its products.

Heinz also bought up other businesses. In 1946, it bought Star-Kist, which made canned tuna products. In 1965, Heinz acquired Ore-Ida and turned it from a regional enterprise to the leading frozen-potato brand in the USA.

An indication of Heinz's deep roots in the UK was the award in 1951 of the Royal Warrant, 'a mark of recognition' for companies that have supplied goods or services for at least five years to a royal household. The queen clearly approved of Heinz baked beans, which was highly prized publicity for the company!

Ore-Ida produces a variety of potato products, including fries and mash.

Workers at the StarKist Tuna Cannery clean the fish before it is tinned.

Along with this expansion came a shift in advertising. Since the 1930s, supermarkets had opened up in wealthy countries, such as the UK and the USA. Now people selected their foods without the guidance of a grocer. Heinz realized the importance of advertising directly to consumers to encourage them to choose its products. In 1955 Heinz products were first advertised on TV in the UK.

TV advertising has always been important to Heinz. This advert was filmed in the 1990s.

Brains
Behind The Brand

R. Burt Gookin
Chief Executive Officer (CEO), 1965–79

R. Burt Gookin was the first non-Heinz family member to become CEO. He is best known for his part in the development of the Universal Product Code (UPC). In 1970 he was appointed chairman of a committee to set up the Uniform Grocery Product Code Council. The group established the UPC, a scanning system for products using barcodes. These now appear on most grocery products worldwide. Barcodes allow companies to track purchases and see which products have run out and which remain unsold. In 1974 Mr Gookin received the Herbert Hoover Award in recognition of his contribution to the development of the UPC.

> " Heinz 57, Heinz 57. You've a family to feed. Heinz have everything you need. Ready when you are, yes indeed. That's Heinz 57! "

Heinz jingle from the 1955 TV advert

Going global from the late 1970s

Heinz continued to grow, buying up other companies and exporting goods to new markets. A big success was the purchase of Weight Watchers International, Inc. in 1978, which produced low-calorie meals. It became the largest weight-loss programme in the USA.

The business experienced challenges, too. From the 1980s, it had to deal with competition from supermarkets' cheaper, own-brand versions of Heinz products. After Anthony O'Reilly became CEO in 1979, he tackled the challenge by cutting costs. Heinz started using thinner glass bottles to lower the cost of production and transport and decreased the size of the StarKist tuna can. It stopped using back labels on bottles to reduce expenses further. With the money saved, O'Reilly spent more on advertising to increase Heinz's market share. Heinz also enlarged its market by expanding in developing countries in the 1980s, forming joint ventures in China and South Korea.

Heinz CEO Anthony O'Reilly poses with a ketchup bottle, 1989.

Cyclists pass a billboard advertising Heinz foods in Fuzhou, China.

In the 1990s, Heinz started to export Heinz Beanz to countries in the East, such as China and Russia, that were keen to buy Western foods. By now, Heinz Beanz were exported to 60 countries – baked beans had gone truly international!

Heinz company directors made careful decisions about which companies to buy and sell, too. In 2002, they sold North American food and pet-food businesses that were not performing well, including StarKist, to the Del Monte Food Company. Heinz bought up profitable companies – HP Sauces and Lea & Perrins Worcestershire Sauce in 2005, and Australian food and drink maker Golden Circle in 2008.

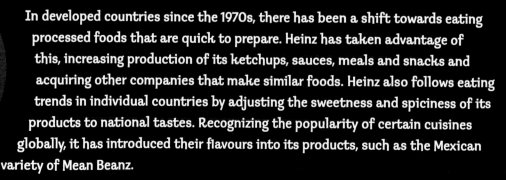

Business Matters $

Following trends in eating habits

In developed countries since the 1970s, there has been a shift towards eating processed foods that are quick to prepare. Heinz has taken advantage of this, increasing production of its ketchups, sauces, meals and snacks and acquiring other companies that make similar foods. Heinz also follows eating trends in individual countries by adjusting the sweetness and spiciness of its products to national tastes. Recognizing the popularity of certain cuisines globally, it has introduced their flavours into its products, such as the Mexican variety of Mean Beanz.

Advertising Heinz

How many Heinz adverts have you seen in supermarkets and the media? Heinz has always invested heavily in advertising. But the rise of the supermarkets, with their wide range of own-brand goods, made advertising even more crucial.

In 1961, Heinz embarked on its biggest advertising campaign yet, giving away 57 Mini-Minor cars, 57 caravans, 57 holidays, and many other prizes, in a soup competition. In 1967, the slogan 'Beanz meanz Heinz' was created and became one of Heinz's best-known advertising slogans. The jingle went, 'A million housewives every day pick up a tin of beans and say: "Beanz meanz Heinz."'

It was followed in 1971 by the 'slowest ketchup in the West.' Slow pouring was an indication of good-quality, thick ketchup. In the 1980s, Heinz urged mums 'not to be mean with the beans'.

The Beanz Meanz Heinz slogan became hugely successful in the 1960s.

All advertising campaigns were designed to keep Heinz goods at the front of people's minds, focusing on the excellent taste and quality of the product in comparison to lower-priced alternatives. By the twenty-first century, this involved promoting products in a variety of media. In 2009, the 'It has to be Heinz' marketing campaign was launched on TV, radio, in-store, online and via public relations (PR) agencies.

Business Matters

$

Heinz also targets its advertising at the food trade as well as individual consumers because its products have always been popular in cafes and fast-food chains. Their soups and baked beans sell extremely well, as do their condiments – everyone loves ketchup on their sausages!

When an advert misfires

Advertising is successful when an advert taps into the popular mood. Viewers identify with the characters in it, which encourages them to buy the product. However, advertisers can misjudge the mood, too. In 2008, Heinz produced an advertisement for its Hellmann's Deli mayo that showed a man giving his male partner a goodbye kiss after making their kids' packed lunches. It believed that a modern audience would accept the same-sex relationship as normal behaviour. However, after 200 complaints from viewers who thought it was 'inappropriate,' Heinz withdrew the advert.

Heinz products are popular with fast-food customers. In Germany, they enjoy Heinz mustard on their sausages.

HEINZ
ESTD 1869 ESTD
SENF
MITTELSCHARF
HEINZ
57 VARIETIES

A wave of innovations

Why do ketchup bottles change size and shape? A company always needs novel products and design innovations to attract new customers and keep up with trends. In 1987, the easy, squeezy plastic bottle was the biggest change since Heinz Ketchup's invention.

In 2003, the famous ketchup bottle was turned upside down, so the cap was at the bottom. But Heinz continued to sell the traditional bottle, so as not to put off any customers who preferred the original style.

The Heinz upside-down bottles alongside the traditional variety.

To fit with customer demand for a choice of environmentally friendly and healthier products, Heinz launched an organic range in 2000 for its main brands, including Organic Tomato Ketchup, Organic Heinz Beanz and Organic Cream of Tomato Soup. It produced a range of organic baby foods containing simple fruit and vegetable blends.

In 2005 Heinz adopted new bean flavours for the first time in 103 years: Mean Beanz, in Mexican, Sweet Chilli and Smokey BBQ varieties, followed by Cheese, Chilli, Garlic and Herbs and Heinz Five Beanz.

Convenience has been proved a significant spur to innovation. In 2007, Snap Pots were devised – individual bean portions that could be cooked in the microwave. The Hoops in Tomato Sauce fridge pack can be resealed so consumers can use just what they need, and it has a see-through measure so they can see exactly how much is left.

Heinz has pushed into specialist markets, too, introducing a gluten-free penne, macaroni and spaghetti range in 2013. Meals especially for kids include Moshi Monster Pasta Shapes and Heinz Mini Meals.

Dutch Crown Prince Willem-Alexander visits the Heinz Innovation Centre at its opening in 2013.

Business Matters

Research and development

The Heinz innovation Centre in Nijmegen, Holland, employs 200 workers who think creatively about new products and packaging. Some teams focus on making Heinz products more convenient for users or more environmentally friendly. Others invent new recipes. To create Heinz Five Beanz, the 'beanz team' held tasting sessions to test a variety of beans for texture, size, colour and taste. Haricot, kidney, borlotti, pinto and cannellini beans were selected. Next the team had to work out the right proportions of each kind to use. They made a sample batch, but found that the kidney beans made the sauce too dark. After reducing the proportion of kidney beans, the recipe was perfect.

'Green' bottles

Like many other companies, Heinz has felt the pressure to 'go green' to play its part in reducing the harm human beings are doing to the environment.

In 2008, CEO Bill Johnson announced nine global sustainability (green) goals, including a promise to reduce the emission of greenhouse gases that cause global warming by one-fifth by 2015. Greenhouse gases are produced by industry, farming and burning fuel – and Heinz is involved in all of these activities.

How could Heinz do this? The main strategy was to bring in more efficient equipment and new technologies.

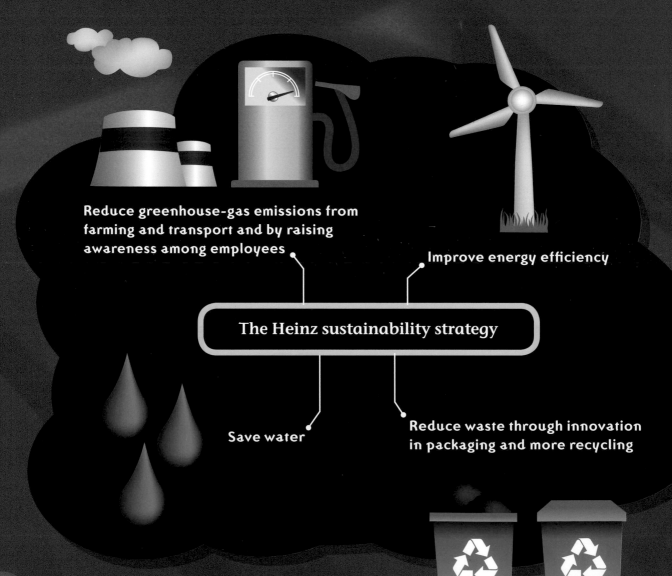

Reduce greenhouse-gas emissions from farming and transport and by raising awareness among employees

Improve energy efficiency

The Heinz sustainability strategy

Save water

Reduce waste through innovation in packaging and more recycling

Heinz's plant bottles are 100 per cent recyclable.

Heinz's plant bottles are 100 per cent recyclable.

Since introducing the top-down bottle in 2003, Heinz has switched to using PET plastic, which saves 10 to 15 per cent of the bottle weight, depending on size. It uses less plastic and the bottles are lighter to transport – lighter loads mean lower fuel costs. The bottles are sourced close to the factories to cut down transport needs. PET plastic is easy to recycle, too. In 2011, Heinz brought in PlantBottle technology – 30 per cent of the plastic in the PET bottle now came from sugar-cane plants, a renewable resource.

Brains

Behind The Brand

Bill Johnson
CEO, 1998–2013

Bill Johnson enjoyed a 31-year career with Heinz, including 15 years as CEO. He began as a marketing manager, becoming president and CEO of Heinz Pet Foods and later StarKist Tuna. He turned around these poorly performing operations and made them profitable. Johnson became President of Heinz in 1996 and CEO in 1998.

His main achievement was to make Heinz a truly global enterprise, expanding its operations in new markets and embracing business on the Internet. He announced the sustainability goals to show that good business could be positive for the environment. Since then, the staff have become engaged in the issues, and the company has continued with the Global Agriculture Program, started in 2000, to encourage more sustainable practices among farms that produce ingredients for Heinz.

Bill Johnson, chairman and chief executive officer of Heinz, in 2010.

Heinz online

Companies today don't just want customers to look at their websites – they want to actively engage with them. By 2012, Heinz had reached 11 million people on social media sites.

Heinz offers games and competitions on Facebook, and the winners receive vouchers to spend on Heinz products. In 2012, when Heinz Five Beanz came out, Heinz ran a fun quiz about how each bean reflected a different personality. In return for the games and activities, the company calls on its fans to promote new products that they're enjoying.

Heinz chefs engage with customers by showing them the best way to cook beans on toast.

Heinz also uses a variety of media to target particular audiences. A site for chefs provides ideas for how to use Heinz soups in their recipes. Soups have QR codes that café and restaurant operators can use to access recipes and menu ideas on their phones. Heinz advertised Dip & Squeeze ketchup to mums to buy at drive-through fast-food outlets because it was easy for kids to use on the go and not messy. It launched a video to boost sales and an app that showed which drive-throughs sold Dip & Squeeze.

Heinz realized it could even take advantage of the time customers are waiting for their food to arrive in a café. At the table, customers can scan a QR code on the Heinz PlantBottle and read all about it.

Brains

Behind The Brand

Brendan Foley
President of Heinz North America
(from 2013)

Brendan Foley has worked in several important positions at Heinz. Always keen to innovate, he designed a bottle that was easy for children to hold with a cap that allowed them to squirt a thin stream of ketchup. As Marketing Director of Global Ketchup and Sauces, Foley was in charge of digital strategy. He saw that the first website Heinz had set up was static – it just provided information. Also, it was pointless having a Facebook page just because other businesses had one. Innovation was key in the social media world. Foley realized that Heinz had to find the best way to engage with its customers and to target different groups of consumers in ways that would appeal to them.

Heinz's Dip and Squeeze ketchup has its own social media sites where fans can share their experiences.

Heinz in the community

An excellent way to promote a business is to be involved in charities that assist communities. The Heinz Charitable Trust supports charities that encourage good nutrition and the health of children and families. Such efforts help to associate the brand with healthy eating.

Through the Heinz Micronutrient Campaign, Heinz works to combat child malnutrition in countries with high levels of poverty, such as Haiti, India, Nigeria and China. Many children suffer from a lack of vitamins, minerals and iron. Heinz distributes sachets of these minerals, which can be mixed into meals. From March to October 2013, Heinz raised money for the project online: for every person who visited the Heinz Micronutrient Campaign webpage, it donated US$1 (62p) to the campaign.

Heinz is helping to fight malnutrition, but is must also bear some responsibility for the health of its own customers. It has been criticized for the high salt content of its sauces and soups. Salt should only be consumed in extremely small quantities, and processed foods tend to contain relatively high amounts. Heinz introduced baked beans with reduced salt and sugar in 2004. Later that decade, US politicians put pressure on big food companies to reduce the salt in all their products. In 2010 Heinz signed the National Salt Reduction Initiative and cut down the salt in its ketchup by 15 per cent.

Heinz includes several healthier options in its range.

Food-safety scandals

In 2013, a serious food-safety scandal erupted in Europe. Some frozen beef products were found to contain horse meat. Heinz checked its products immediately and stated that it was confident that its food supplies were pure. The same year, Brazil banned sales of a batch of Heinz tomato ketchup made in Mexico after traces of rat fur were detected. Heinz rapidly mounted an investigation. It is essential for companies to take breaches of food safety seriously and reassure customers that the products they buy are safe. Failure to do so can destroy brand loyalty, and customers may switch to another brand.

Heinz regularly checks all of its products in food safety laboratories.

Heinz: the largest takeover in history

Heinz is a huge enterprise, but in 2013 it was bought by even bigger businesses. Multinational company Berkshire Hathaway and investment firm 3G Capital took over Heinz for US$28 billion (£17.5 billion) – the largest-ever takeover deal in the food industry.

Warren Buffett, who owned Berkshire Hathaway, was one of the richest men in the world and his business owned international burger chain Burger King. At the time, Heinz sold its ketchup to many of Burger King's competitors, including McDonald's.

Burger King Worldwide CEO Bernardo Hees became CEO of Heinz while remaining the vice-chairman of the board of Burger King. McDonald's did not want to buy from a rival company and decided to stop using Heinz ketchup in its outlets.

WILLIAM R. JOHNSON

It is our kind of company. I've sampled it many times. Any time we see a deal is attractive and it's our kind of business and we've got the money, I'm ready to go.

Mr Buffett at the time of the takeover deal, February 2013

Heinz CEO Bill Johnson (left) and Alex Behring from 3G Capital announce the takeover deal, 2013.

The purchasing companies took on US$12.6 billion (£7.9 billion) of debt to buy Heinz. To offset the debt, they reduced Heinz's budget: 11 senior managers lost their jobs; 600 posts were cut in offices in the USA and Canada, and budget cuts at the Heinz offices were introduced, too. In early 2014, it was announced that two Heinz plants in Europe would close down.

The new management of Heinz did not make immediate changes to the products, although there would no doubt be innovations in the future. Given the huge brand loyalty to Heinz, it appeared likely that the company would continue to produce its popular sauces, snacks and meals as it had done so successfully for over 100 years.

Bernardo Hees (left) brought in cost-cutting measures at Heinz as he had at Burger King.

Business Matters

Job cuts

When a business buys a new enterprise, it usually has to borrow money for the purchase and pay interest on the loan. Yet it wants to make as much profit as possible after absorbing the new company. The easiest way to increase profits is to drive down costs by cutting jobs. For example, it may be possible to combine departments such as Human Resources and Accounts, using fewer staff. This is why job cuts often follow a takeover.

Design your own Heinz venture

To create a new product, it is helpful to put together a product development brief like the one below. This is a sample brief for 'Add your own Heinz flavour' sachets.

The SWOT analysis on the page opposite can help you to think about the strengths and weaknesses of your product, and the opportunities and threats presented. This helps you to see how practical your idea is before you think of investing in it.

Product Development Brief

Name of product: Add your own Heinz flavour

The product explained (use 25 words or less):
A range of sachets to add to your Heinz Beanz or Heinz Ketchup and make up your own delicious flavour.

Target age of consumers: All ages.

What is the product?: This range of sachets has different flavours, such as Mexican, Thai curry, Indian curry and sweet and sour, in a powder that customers can add to their Heinz sauces and meals.

Are there any similar products available?: None that I know of.

What makes your product different?: It's a new way for consumers to customize their Heinz products.

SWOT Analysis
(Strengths, Weaknesses, Opportunities and Threats)

Name of product you are assessing ...
Add your own Heinz flavour

The information below will help you assess the venture. By addressing all four areas, you can make your product stronger and more likely to be a success.

Questions to consider

Does your product do something unique?

What are its USPs? (unique selling points)

Strengths
Yes. No other product allows you to add your own flavours to beans, ketchup and other Heinz products quickly, cheaply and easily.

This idea is like the Coca-Cola Freestyle vending machine that allows you to create your own flavour of soft drink, but applied for the first time to Heinz foods.

Why wouldn't people buy this range?

Does it live up to the claims you make?

Weaknesses
People like the existing range of Heinz flavours and may not want to buy additional flavours.

The range would need to be tried out on focus groups to check that the best flavours have been selected. If the flavours include salt and sugar, they would make the products less healthy and go against Heinz's efforts to reduce salt and sugar in their meals and sauces.

Can the range be expanded in the future?

Will new markets emerge for this range?

Opportunities
Yes. If the range proves popular, it will be relatively easy to expand it.

The sachets can be marketed in all areas where Heinz products are sold.

Is there really a need to add flavours to Heinz products when there is already such a good range available?

Is it the right time to launch the new range?

Are any of the weaknesses so bad that they might affect the success of the venture in the long term?

Threats
Although the sachets will be small and low-cost, consumers may not want to pay the additional price to add a new flavour.

Heinz has already greatly expanded its range in recent years and it may not be the right time to add a new range.

None of the weaknesses are particularly bad. Heinz already has huge production and sales capacity so the risks of producing a small range to test the waters are not great.

Do you have the skills Heinz needs?
Try this quiz!

1) It's lunchtime and there's not much in the fridge. What do you do?

a) Wait for someone else to make your lunch.

b) Eat a slice of toast – you're not that hungry anyway.

c) Make an imaginative sandwich with leftovers and sauces in the cupboard.

2) You're eating a meal in a café and the food is rather dull and tasteless. What are you thinking?

a) It's OK, it will fill me up till Dad cooks dinner tonight.

b) I'll douse the whole lot in ketchup and it'll taste better.

c) With a few added flavours, all these items would be tastier – and you know exactly which ones would help.

3) You're working on a group project in class and everyone is fighting over how to do it. What do you do?

a) Join the fight – you think you're right!

b) Get the teacher to come and sort it out.

c) Tell everyone to be quiet, ask everyone to give their point of view and then vote on the best way to do the project.

4) You finally work out how to do the class project but no one is doing their work. What do you do now?

a) Well, if no one else is bothering, why should you?

b) Do your part of the work – you don't want to get into trouble.

c) Work out a plan so that everyone has one part of the project to do and ask them to do it – now!

5) It's your best friend's party tomorrow, but you also have a mountain of homework. How do you cope?

a) It's a no-brainer – you head to the party.

b) You go to the party and work out a complicated excuse to explain why you didn't do the homework.

c) You get up super-early the next day, complete the homework and then go to the party.

6) You're at the party at a burger restaurant and you squirt ketchup all over the table by mistake. What's your plan?

a) You shove some paper napkins over the top and hope no one notices.

b) You clean up the mess carefully and move the bottle out of the way.

c) After cleaning up the mess, you examine the ketchup bottle and wonder how the cap could be improved so the ketchup doesn't squirt all over the place.

Results

Mostly As: You are focusing on what's happening now. Why not think ahead and start trying to develop the skills you'll need when you're older, such as teamwork?

Mostly Bs: You certainly do your bit and have some initiative. If you're interested in the food-processing business, you might like to take up cooking or study food technology at school.

Mostly Cs: Seems like you have a flair for teamwork and some leadership skills already, as well as some interest in food processing. Work on your cooking, study hard at school and maybe one day you'll work for Heinz!

Glossary

brand a product made by a particular company under a particular name

brand loyalty when customers continue to buy the same brand because they have decided that it is a quality product and prefer it to other similar products

Chief Executive Officer the person in a company who has the most power

condiment a substance such as salt or sauce that is used to give flavour to food

debt a sum of money that somebody owes

Depression a period when there is little economic activity and many people are poor or without jobs

emission gas or other substance that is sent out into the air

environmentally friendly something that does not harm the environment

export to sell and send goods to another country

global warming the increase in temperature of the Earth's atmosphere that is caused by the increase of particular gases, especially carbon dioxide

gluten-free without a sticky substance that is a mixture of two proteins and is left when starch is removed from flour, especially wheat flour. Gluten makes some people ill, so they have to eat products without it

greenhouse gases any of the gases that are thought to cause the warming of the Earth, especially carbon dioxide

headquarters the place from which an organization controls its work

innovation the introduction of new things, ideas or ways of doing something

interest the extra money that you pay back when you borrow money or that you receive when you lend money

investment firm a company that puts money into buying companies that it believes will be successful

malnutrition poor health caused by a lack of food or a lack of the right types of food, for example, vitamins and minerals

marketing promoting and selling goods or services, including advertising and market research (finding out what customers want)

organic produced without using artificial chemicals

PET a plastic used for food and drink containers

processed when a raw food is treated in a factory in order to make a new product, for example, fresh tomatoes are processed to make tomato ketchup

production line a line of workers and machines in a factory, along which a product passes until it is finished

profit the money a company makes from selling its goods, after paying the costs of producing them

promote to help to sell a product or make it more popular by advertising it or offering it at a special price

promotional materials materials connected to advertising, such as banners and posters

public company the public can buy shares in a public company so that they own part of it, rather than it being owned by one person or family

publicity the business of attracting the attention of the public to something, such as a product or a company

renewable a resource that is replaced naturally and can be used without the risk of finishing it all

subsidiary a company that is controlled by another company because that other company owns the majority of the shares in it

sustainability using natural products and energy in a way that does not harm the environment

Index

BIG BU$INE$$

Contents of titles in this series:

More titles in the Big Business series